CN00945644

PENGUIN MODERN CLASSICS

Down in the Valley

Laurie Lee has written some of the best-loved travel books in the English language. Born in Stroud, Gloucestershire, in 1914, he was educated at Slad village school and Stroud Central School. At the age of nineteen he walked to London and then travelled on foot through Spain, where he was trapped by the outbreak of the Civil War. He later returned by crossing the Pyrenees, as he recounted in *A Moment of War.*

Laurie Lee published four collections of poems: *The Sun My Monument* (1944), *The Bloom of Candles* (1947), *My Many-Coated Man* (1955) and *Pocket Poems* (1960). His other works include *The Voyage of Magellan* (1948), *The Firstborn* (1964), *I Can't Stay Long* (1975), and *Two Women* (1983). He also wrote three bestselling volumes of autobiography: *Cider with Rosie* (1959), which has sold over six million copies worldwide, *As I Walked Out One Midsummer Morning* (1969) and *A Moment of War* (1991).

David Parker was born in Stoke on Trent. He is a television programme maker and author. His work for television includes many films about aspects of life in twentieth-century Britain. He is the author of two books about Exmoor and is currently working on one about the Second World War and one about Britain's steam railway revival. He lives in Bristol.

LAURIE LEE

Down in the Valley

A Writer's Landscape

Edited by David Parker

PENGUIN BOOKS

PENGUIN CLASSICS

UK | USA | Canada | Ireland | Australia
India | New Zealand | South Africa

Penguin Classics is part of the Penguin Random House group of companies whose addresses can be found at global.penguinrandomhouse.com

First published 2019
001

Set in 13.2/16 pt Dante MT Std by Integra Software Services Pvt. Ltd, Pondicherry
Printed in Great Britain by Clays Ltd, Elcograf S.p.A.

A CIP catalogue record for this book is available from the British Library

ISBN: 978–0–241–41167–4

For Wendy

Contents

1. *The Village Pond* 1
2. *Telling a Story* 15
3. *The Church, Miserden* 25
4. *Bulls Cross* 32
5. *The Violin on the Wall* 43
6. *The Village School* 55
7. *The Woolpack* 61
8. *Home* 73
9. *Swift's Hill* 86

Afterword by David Parker 97

I

The Village Pond

This is our village pond, it's on the edge of Slad, down at the bottom of the village. It was where we kids gathered for fun, games and secrecy.

This was our kingdom, the centre of all our juvenile recreations: summer bathing, winter skating and general gathering together to experiment with the first pulsations of sensual enjoyments.

We called it Squire Jones's pond. The squire glorified in having this ancestral, almost feudal possession of this place but he never checked on us, and we could do whatever we wished. Since then it's had some posts and fencing put up to keep people out but we don't take any notice of them. These fences were put in by quite a nice man but the previous owner put up the sort of wire that went round it like the Berlin Wall and the villagers used to come down in the night with big wire cutters. So that didn't endure for very long. It's still a free gathering place. It's inhabited by coots and moorhens and dabchicks.

I don't remember ever coming down and looking at a dabchick. But the coots were very close, bosom chums of mine. We used to spend many a happy hour together. These are the sort of things I remember and we still come down here. In the summer there are great flotations of pink lilies. They are a month behind this year. Aren't we all! But they'll be out by the end of June and they're just like great stars of pink candle wax, floating on the water.

It was at the village pond where almost everything happened in terms of games, village gossip, childish errors. It was a teeming little paradise of wildlife and very few people except we kids came here and I think we were tolerated by the wildlife because they, and the horses in the field, it was the only life they knew. They got used to us. In summer we'd swim, and in winter skate and fall through the ice, chase each other, steal the moorhens' eggs, get attacked by the swans. And they are pretty difficult to cope with when you are a kid, because they have these huge wings and they would come like Concorde taking off. They'd come across us and bash into us and we used to scream and jump into the hedges.

There was one macabre, dramatic occasion that took place at this pond. The milkman, Fred Bates, the young man bringing the milk up to our cottage, one morning was late. One of my sisters asked him:

'What kept you, Fred Bates, what happened?'

And he said, 'I seen her.'

'Who?'

'Miss Flynn.'

'What happened to her?' my sister asked.

'Well, I was coming past the pond and there was what looked like a dead swan, I thought that's a dead swan and went over and had a look at it, and it was Miss Flynn. She was looking up at me with her eyes wide open and her hair all loose. And there was not a stitch on her, and she was drowned. And I dropped me bucket and I ran up here.'

And my sister said, 'You'd better have a cup of tea.'

'Well, I've had about five already.'

Because he'd been telling the story all round the village. So he became a bit of a hero. But we came down here and the women were gathered around the pond; the village women who'd heard the story. They'd already taken her body away on a hurdle, and there was a sheen of milk still on the pond where Fred had dropped his churn. And I remember thinking as the women were chatting between themselves, 'Miss Flynn, poor Miss Flynn, you wouldn't think, I only saw her a couple of days ago, she was down in Stroud in the Home and Colonial and she said to me and I said good morning Miss Flynn and she said good morning like she often does . . .'

And I thought, all this talk, is this what happens when you die? Do they say, I saw you in the Home and Colonial? Miss Flynn was a sort of Gabriel Rossetti heroine, a tragic young girl. I never understood what was behind it all but I do remember thinking – I was about eight at the time – that's where Miss Flynn came down in the night, lay down in the pond and pulled the water over her head, and drowned.

But I think that this place would appeal, I didn't realize it then, it would appeal to all the Victorian painters with Ophelias. Everywhere you went there were Ophelias floating by, covered with wild flowers. And if it wasn't Ophelia it was Edna or Bertha or possibly Rosie. And it all centred on this little pond. Though it's not so little now. We're better off for a village pond than many villages round here. Anyway, it's a gathering place and I come back here continuously, to refresh myself.

It isn't a natural pond; it's a millpond, built in order to run one of the mills across the road, across the lane here. There used to be about eight mills, all with banked-up ponds. The stream runs over there, to get enough head, enough power, to turn the mills' wheels. At one end is a dam, it used to be built up. The stream which runs past the pond would have been dammed up to about six feet. This water in the pond would have been held in order to feed the mill, the cloth mill, which is just down the bank there, Steanbridge mill. The whole of this valley was a series of stepping stones of cloth mills, run off these streams, but you'll find there were stockades and dams of water all along the valleys and this is one of the few left. The others were washed away in a great cloudburst, a flood, in about 1860. They were all just swept off the face of the earth, but this one still remains, thank goodness. It remains as a legacy. We were spared. Lloyds are still paying for it but how grateful we are for it, because there is nothing up in Slad village itself that is more liquified than The Woolpack inn.

Sheep were grazed on the hills. They would be driven down to this stream and further up there's a sheep wash where they used to have their fleece washed and disinfected. They were then sheared in the early part of the year, the wool taken from them, would be put on mule trains that would go down the valley to the weaving mills of Stroud. The Stroud mills were famous for their military scarlet and for their green baize. So they were responsible for not only the snooker player Steve Davis's great victories, because they made the green baize for the billiard tables, but some of the greatest defeats in British military history. When soldiers appeared in the Light Brigade they were all in this scarlet, as if saying to the enemy, 'Look at me, I'm here.' So the old Turks just mowed them down, alas. Very sad in those days, but they all wear Raglan coats now, that's the new camouflage.

Stroud was well known for its worsted. Many of the great houses round here and the gorgeous churches, going back to the sixteenth century, were built on the fortunes of the wool trade. And we haven't given up entirely. We've got a showroom in Bond Street, of wool from Stroud. Something happened in these valleys that conspired to make it a perfect place for growing wool. There is a wonderful local breed of sheep, very fleecy. All the pubs round here are called The Woolpack, or The Fleece Inn, showing how important wool was to us. There was a thing for teasing the wool, working on the nap, the cloth. And these teazles were just growing in the hedgerows and they had little hooks on them, they didn't grow anywhere else. They just grew for us, we were blessed on all sides.

Below our place in Slad you'll find sloping hills, terraced fields where they used to stretch the cloth to dry in the sun, and many of the old houses had little factories in the loft where the peasants used to gather and work for a penny a day. Squire Jones still has this great workshop. I don't think his descendants make cloth any more but it's all there and the way things are going, if we get into industrial trouble and need to pull our socks up, worsted socks, I think maybe some of the old mills will be regenerated. Let's see how we get on with Europe. Anyway we are all ready to go in this valley. And all the way down, there were eighteen mills going down into Stroud, and beautiful they were too, beautifully built.

There are five valleys leading to Stroud. They are like five fingers on a hand and Stroud will be in the middle. There's Painswick, Slad, Chalford, and two others which shall be nameless because they are chapel and we're church, so we don't talk about them.* They were all fed from streams which concentrated on Stroud. The stream was the motive power. The stream was what turned the machinery in the

* The 'chapel' valleys are Ruscombe and Nailsworth.

cloth mills and it was extremely valuable. As I say, we're still here. When the nation calls we're ready to go back to our old trade, which was the greatest in the West Country. I'm ready to tease anybody who wants to come round to be teased, lay them on one of the terraced slopes. Lay them out to tease them first, then lay them out to dry.

My village, Slad, never had much history but there was one memorable moment that we still boast about a lot and that was when King Charles, in the Civil War, marched down from Bisley, which is two miles over the hill. He marched down this lane, up over Bulls Cross and into Painswick, where he stabled his horses in the church. That got him into a lot of local trouble. He went down into Gloucester, which was under siege; he went down to try and join up with some friends, some Cavaliers.

He was defeated, kicked out and came back over the hill, over Bulls Cross where there are a lot of small ditches, and where – we like to pretend – they buried many of his defeated troops. And down at the bottom of the crossroads there used to be an oak tree, until quite recently, where he was supposed to have hidden. Anyway, there's a myth going all over south-west England, 'King Charles's oak', lots of places claim their oak was where the king hid. But if any oak was the real oak that Charles hid in, it was this one, across the lane.

Just down here by the stream there used to be a gathering place for us kids from the village to come and play on summer evenings. This was where the sheep wash was: a stone bath, cut from stone, and a stone bridge.

They used to bring the sheep down from the hills to be washed before they were sheared in the spring. Sheep bleating; it's a lovely sound, even I can hear that. I can still remember the voices of kids in the village. 'See you in the sheep wash, coming down the sheep wash, Laurie, coming down the sheep wash?'

Can you imagine the excitement of the sheep wash? We couldn't see properly. But what a bliss it was. The girls, the summer, paddling, pulling up their skirts, shrieks of laughter and all the innocence of wild water on naked skin, warmth. You must not be too free with your language, you just say to Kate, 'Didn't turn up then, what kept yer? You were supposed to be here at twelve!' I said I'll see you in the sheep wash on a summer's day, midsummer's day, and we'll have a romp in the bubbling, turbulent waters. It's about time I picked fluff off my shroud I think, climbed into my grave and pulled the wood over me, I'm getting carried away. It's just public-bar reminiscences.

This lane next to us is still passable just, but the banks of it are about twenty or thirty feet deep; it's cut so deeply into the hill by the passage of traffic, footsteps, cartwheels, sheep, and they've dug down through the generations. I think it's about a thousand years old. It leads up to Bisley and Bisley is one of the oldest towns on the Cotswolds. It's where Jilly Cooper lives now. It's a rotten place for writers round here, well it's not rotten but they gather round here because at any moment they may have to shin up an oak tree; they're always being chased around, being defeated by their publishers.

Bisley is a beautiful stone village. It's about a thousand feet high and the wind blows in from the, I nearly said urinals, the winds blow in from the Urals. It's terribly cold and a local saying still is, 'Where was yer born then? Born in Bisley was yer? Go and shut the bloody door.'

There are two ways of travelling in these valleys. Either you went along the top from the local town, the old highways, literally high ways. The old roads ran along the tops of the hills to keep away from the marshes and the bogs and the streams. Then they'd cut a lane across, diagonally across the valley as this one was, diagonally across instead of going all the way round, across a little stone bridge and you'll find a number of rectangular lanes that are alternatives to the high ways. There is the Bisley road from Stroud, which is right up on the top, and there is another one which comes out by Bulls Cross, which is the intersection of about five highways from Painswick and Stroud. This road was open until quite recently, but it would be very difficult to get up there now without doing in your car. There are fallen trees and rocks and abandoned cavaliers, cannon, armour: fossilized tears.

This place is called Steanbridge and everybody said it was named after a squire, Stevens, 'Steven's Bridge'. But I know and my mother knew that's just pomp, vanity. It's Stone Bridge, because stone bridges were very unusual. You usually forded a steam. But this one was a stone bridge, a bridge made of stone, and therefore something to boast about. So I think the origin of Steanbridge is 'stone bridge' and I'm going to stick with that.

On a Saturday morning, you'd hear the jackal cries of the boys and the shrieks of the girls being pursued over the common and down the lanes. It was all part of wildlife and nature. The kids don't come out any more: they are watching bloody *Neighbours* on television I suspect.

Now they are all locked up in their little rooms on computers and of course there aren't as many children as there once were, there are motor cars instead. Whereas once the parents used to send their children out to play, now they come out and wash their cars.

To me, the disappearing voices of children is one of the impoverishments of country life. They are fading, in their electronic prisons – but that's a complaint that one falls into most easily, when you are a geriatric: saying how much better it was in the old days. Well actually, I'd like a computer myself, because I believe there are things you can do with a computer which we didn't dare do in those days, such as certain fantasies that you can organize. Those pleasures have come too late. Can't see, can't even read the small print on the back of *Private Eye* any more, my eyes have gone.

Up there is the field where I tumbled with Rosie and that is still the same. We used to meet, the community that is, for village recreations which would be held up in that wood and below the wood in that field. Swings in the trees, races and games up and down and then a tea in the village hut. Twelve teapots, polished and waiting for us with what we called 'fly cake', piles of fly cake. And this was a treat that would last.

We only ate sweets once a week. One sweet that my sister brought home. Not one every five minutes. Here I go again complaining about the young. I would relish just one day of life's sensuous extravaganza that kids are allowed now to indulge in. I think by the time they are twelve or fifteen they are past it. They are exhausted. No wonder they want to relax in their room with their computer. They are probably writing their memoirs by the time they are eleven or twelve and saying, 'If I had my time over again.'

But this to me is a homeland to which I return. To which I have to return, and can't imagine another life without being here. It's old. It goes back to the Stone Age. There are Stone Age forts all along the top of the escarpment. There's Haresfield, Painswick Beacon, there's Crickley Hill up near Birdlip, where they found the old Bronze Age queen's mirror which is now in the British Museum. We want it back, by the way. We want it in Stroud Museum. We have a call for that Bronze Age mirror, in perfect order, dug up near Birdlip. We understand about the Elgin Marbles, we want that Bronze Age mirror brought back, thank you very much. And the villages around: Camp, Bisley, Miserden, they all have these old burial grounds, where the Bronze Age chieftains were buried, and those tumps in the fields which you still see, untroubled, untouched still, are in a certain way inviolate, sacred. No farmer for centuries has touched them, they always plough round them, they don't disturb them, they don't disturb the sleeping giants.

And this is one of the reasons, apart from its splendour, its beauty, in season and out, it's one of the reasons that I feel I've inherited, just by being here, inherited this ancient, pre-Roman and pre-Iron Age, almost pre-Stone Age civilization. And I do my best to carry it on, with all its ravages and contentments; which are many.

2

Telling a Story

True darkness, that I do remember in the village, and true silence. Today you can never get far from the noise of the road or an electric light. As a child I could get around the village almost by touch and the darkness was unbroken. You could see the stars close to you. These days, two fields away, or two roads away, there is constant traffic, which I associated with the first time I went to London when I was about seventeen. This roar of traffic I had never heard before and I thought extraordinary. Now it's something we take for granted, always somebody, somewhere has got an engine working. If it isn't a car it's a microwave.

My village was a church village. All through the seasons, social life and community life revolved around the church. There was Easter, Ascension Day, some

Christian festivals and some pagan festivals. They were all part of the church. And our lives were influenced very much by the King James Bible, it was part of our vocabulary, part of our natural exchange of language at that time, and I was very much a believer. I'd say prayers on my knees until I was about fifteen. 'God bless the king, friends and relations, make me a good boy,' and all that stuff. I would not put up with any nonsense. No infidels came my way without a rebuff.

And then one day, on the way back from Painswick where I'd been off to pay the rates; we used to pay the rates in the town hall. We'd run across Greenhouse Lane, a steep lane, with great banks on each side. I was on my way back coming up to Bulls Cross and through my mind went lines from the King James Bible.

'And God visited the sins of the fathers, and to the third and the fourth generation of them that hate him, and he said that I will show mercy onto thousands of them who love me and keep my commandments.'

And I thought, this is not a God that one should admire, this is an old tribal bully, laying down vengeance for those who hate and those who love, the third and fourth generation. And that was the moment, I remember vividly, just where I was when this kind of revelation came to me. I gave up God from then on.

I still took Jesus. Christ became a man, a teacher, a prophet who I have learned to live by, and his teaching, ever since. I have respect for him, but for God and the people who use God nowadays as an excuse for all their evils and temptations and over-indulgences, he's out as far as I'm concerned.

'God is an old tribal bully,' I said. 'He's a voice from the Old Testament and I'll have no more to do with him.' It lifted such a weight from my mind, though ever since that moment I have never been able to use God as an excuse.

But so far as the Bible is concerned, I feel that the enrichment of language which the Old Testament, as well as the New, gave us was so important to our ways of reacting to life, to the seasons, to our relationships, our goals, our ambitions.

The language was so rich, I think that one of the great, one of the most diabolical, changes that I cannot really forgive, is the pollution of the modern translation. Pollution is a word I use almost deliberately. The richness of the King James Bible, which was a public gift from the early scriptures, and whose unforgettable images that we learned and were brought up with, have all gone. The language I now hear in morning service I find is, it's scaled down to a platitudinous voice of, forgive me for saying this, but of building-society managers, suburban bank clerks or insurance salesmen.

There is one passage in the King James Bible which says that when a man was cured by Christ, he'd been brought on a stretcher and brought down to Christ, they begged that he should cure him and Christ laid his hand on him and he said, 'Arise, take up thy bed and walk.' Now in those few short epithets is an occurrence of suggestions; 'arise' does not just mean 'arise'. I don't have to tell you this, any old country vicar would tell you what 'arise' meant. But the new version says, 'Get up, pick up your bed and go home.' It just sounds like the local policeman arresting you for drunkenness, you lying in the gutter. It is not the gentle, healing voice that Christ used in the New Testament and set the man on his feet, and not just on his feet but on the road to a future belief, expectation. And it is brutally dull.

So that is why I resent, no, why I grieve for the passing of the King James version. I've written to the bishop. He replied, but instead of saying, in reverential fashion,

'Dear son, I hold your thoughts close to my mind and close to my soul, and I will pray for you and ask your forgiveness,' instead of that he replied, in the tone of an officious bank clerk,

'Dear Mr Lee, your opinions have been noted. Yours, Cantab.'

Cantab, ugh.

If I wish to be buried at church I must say no more. Otherwise I shall be unforgiven. I was listening to a young woman on the radio on Sunday morning. They have half an hour on Radio Four. Half an hour of scripture problems, of faith problems, people arguing about the coming of female priests. The interviewer asked the young woman,

'Have you always had the ambition to join the church, and become a priest?' 'Oh no, I'm very keen on horses and I like tennis very much and very keen on travel and heuristics and then one day God touched my button, and I joined the church.'

And I thought, is it as easy as that, God touches your button?

But that phrase, 'God touched my button', left me wondering, hasn't he got other things to do, the unbelievers to destroy and massacre in the deserts of Sinai? He's got a lot of bullying to do.

★

But as for the inspiration for my writing, I suppose it comes to revisiting the sensations, the smells, the adventures of my life.

I went away as a young man. I was away for twenty years and when I came back to Slad I was waking in the morning from a very heavy, dreamy, drugged sleep. And as I was waking I heard a blackbird singing, I had forgotten I had left the village and I thought, he sounds like a Gloucestershire blackbird; he sounds like a Slad blackbird.

And then, when I was fully awake, I realized it *was* a Slad blackbird; it *was* a Gloucestershire blackbird. I had not heard it for twenty years but it was instantly recognizable because they mimic their fathers and mothers. Just as we mimic our fathers and our mothers and our grandparents, these birds will come back to the same wood, same field, same hedgerow and nest where their parents nested and are brought up by their parents. They have been flying back to Slad, and God bless them, it's a good place to fly back to, they mimic their parents. So, naturally they have a Gloucestershire accent.

But you asked me this specific question: 'Putting it down on paper, where did that come from?' I think it is easily understandable so far as I'm concerned. All my beginnings were hatched into this very compact series of narrow, brief valleys, which are like seed pods. They collected the seasons of the year around them and in which, as I have tried to describe, they were the same but were different. There was a winter Slad and there was a summer Slad and they were almost different countries, because the qualities of that particular season would inhabit that particular valley. All our ways of living and growing, our nourishments, would depend on the time of the year.

I was lucky in having this very rich start in life and was never out of touch with the community. Better than any soap opera. This script that I was living and enjoying, was sharing with my neighbours, wasn't a product of an exhausted scriptwriter, beer-stained instead of tear-stained, by someone who was recycling, for money, some second-hand experiences that he picked up from a mate of his somewhere up the Old Kent Road. No, what we were sharing was certainly a thousand years old perhaps and the habits, the greatness, the goodness and the evil and the sins and the hungers and the habits of relying on each other for help were natural to us, and natural to these parts. And I was thinking the other day that all the families, all the names of the families which are descended from, are scattered around here like little herbs. It sounds a bit whimsical but it isn't so. You had the Greens, the Wrights, the Hoggs, the Webbs, the

Carters, the Gardners, the Lights. My grandfather was a Light. Very snobby he was. He would say, 'We are the oldest family in the Bible. God said, Let there be light, and there was light! And that was long before Adam.'

When I had my change of faith, I used to tease him. I'd ask:

'Did God say, Let there be light?'

'That's right, boy, Let there be light.'

'And darkness covered the face of the world,' I replied and I thought, that taught him.

My mother was a self-taught reader. She was someone who should have had a better education; she had to leave school when she was thirteen because her mother died and she had to look after her brothers. So she never quite made it. Though she was full of tastes and love for literature that she could get round to. She described to me her teacher's grief and despair when she had to leave school. The teacher had told her that she was a wonderful girl, she had a wonderful head. She was very scatty, my mother, but she could tell a story. Mother, you could tell a marvellous story. 'Had me in fits,' she'd say, 'had me in fits.'

But then everybody could, I reckon in the village, because we were brought up on this particular diet, this food, of the Old Testament and the Prayer Book.

We had no wireless, no television, and no newspapers, the older souls couldn't read. Because of that start, I suppose many of the villagers, who you can still hear around, began by not being able to read. They had very compact vocabularies but they told stories with such command of their vocabulary, perhaps 200 to 500 words, they never had to hesitate and grab and use second-hand clichés, 'at the end of the day', 'we must have a level playing field', 'having said that', and all this jargon you get with second-hand Westminster, Palace of Westminster, and Westminster Abbey: unfortunately, they speak the same language now. But to have that command of language that these valley people had! They could tell a story just as the mariners in Homer's day must have been able to tell, with a complete command of a very effective vocabulary, born in them, nourished in them as they grew up. They could set your hair on end, retelling the old dramas of the valleys.

These days, to tell a story, it's either second hand or chock-full of frustrations and incoherences or clichés. I have tried to do my best to keep away from that because I realized that in telling a story, if you use somebody else's language people are not going to be interested. They are not going to read it. Try and describe something as you are looking at it and engage their attention. By telling them what it was like to see this for the first time as a boy, or read it aloud, or have it read to them, they'll not only say, 'Yes, I know what he means,' but then they will write me a letter saying, 'It brought back my childhood you know, it's just how I felt.' And I am so pleased to feel that I have touched a lot of tendril remembrances in their past. They may be living north of the border, in Wales, or elsewhere. We all share the same beginnings.

And I felt I was lucky perhaps, though it was a struggle, when I wrote very slowly, and still do, but it was something that I was able to do deliberately, because I wouldn't read a book written in a style which included lines like 'The garden was a blaze of colour.' All right, well having said that, that's a seed package you can buy in Woolworths, but you have got to say exactly what you mean by a 'blaze of colour'. You have to reinterpret it, recycle it, reawaken it. This woman was talking and she said, 'Something snapped in my brain.' She didn't say what it was, but we know what it was, don't we? It was the perished elastic of a misused understanding, that's what snapped in her brain.

3

The Church, Miserden

This is the grave of my old chum Frank Mansell in Miserden churchyard, quite near to where he was brought up. We had some grand times together. He was a remarkable fellow, very Cotswold, Cotswold as a dry stone wall. Rugged, windswept, honest, rooted in these hills. He was also a strange mixture, he was a workman, he worked for the post office, he was an astrologer, he was a demon bowler in the local cricket team at Sheepscombe, and he had a feeling for these stones. He was a marvellous local poet.

He showed me some of his ballads, as he called them, when I first came back to Slad. We used to meet in the pub and go through each other's work. And his poetry was so direct and so local and so genuine, innocent and strong, like him, that we thought we could get it published. So we got together and between us we set up a publishing firm called the Wittantree Tree Press. It was named after an old tree, a windswept tree, which is bent from the west to the east by the prevailing wind. He always felt that the way he walked bore that kind of windswept look about it. And he was absolutely right. It was mostly an inclination from the west to the east which inclined his huge muscular body to the prevailing wind. But as well as that, coming back from the pub in Bisley, after his drink, which was known as Old Peculier, this gave him that sort of inclination. An inclination which I shared.

So we got this little printer down in Cainscross and we set him up with a little paperback. Then, when we had printed off 2,000, we'd go round the pubs with a little box of these and we'd stick them around the bar. And he sold all 2,000, which was almost unheard of, even for a well-known London poet to sell 2,000. Frank sold 2,000 just around the countryside, mostly in the pubs. We had a second printing, and he went into hardback. And at that stage I began to get rather jealous, but I swallowed my pride and enjoyed the fact that we were living off, drinking, our profits as we went around.

And I remember his voice, he read his poems as naturally as birdsong and I can remember them now.

I read one at his funeral, 'Cotswold Choice'. My eyes are going, I can't read them now but I can hear him, under this tree, and among these stone walls, I can hear his voice saying:

> From Wittantree tree and Througham
>   fields,
> from Miserden and Slad
> grand would I walk through summer
> and happy times I've had.

Frank, you'll forgive me not being able to remember your verse with all its natural glory, I'm making it up a bit and editing it as I go along, t'wasn't half as good as your original, Frank. See you later in the Butcher's Arms. Sleep well, old lad.

He died young, at 60. I saw him the day before he died and I've got a recording of him telling me of a quick way to go from Slad to a pub that was up on the top on the other side of Minchinhampton. And he was telling me about all the shortcuts and all the lanes. I thought I knew them all but he was just telling me, very slumberously, because he was quite ill then. But in this very rough, eloquent, Cotswold voice, he told me how to get from Slad to Tetbury and from Tetbury to Minchinhampton and from

Minchinhampton to this pub he wanted me to go to the next day and check up on the sales. But the next day his friend rang me up early in the morning. He had died in the morning, very suddenly, not of the disease with which he was pressed by but something quite different, coronary heart. And he was buried here. And he was so well known, we had a church full and people gathered in the churchyard.

He lived in a little cottage. When we were coming up from Sheepscombe to Miserden and where we are now, there is a crossroads and a little cottage called the Salt Box. In the old days there were salt mines around Droitwich. And they would bring the salt, on packhorses, down over the hills, over Birdlip and across this top road to the Salt Box, where they used to change their horses and take the salt on down to Sharpness, and export it along the River Severn. And so we'd tease him for living in a salt box: peppery old character, but never mind, he was very proud of it and so were we. He is remembered as lord of the manor of the Salt Box, Sheepscombe.

He lived there, alone for most of the time I knew him. He ran a little vegetable garden and wrote these long astrological predications for old ladies. They used to send him a note saying, can you prophesy what is going to happen?

Seriously, he would write down their birth date, and sheets of paper would go out very carefully composed, spinning the most unlikely futures for these old dears. But he believed in it and they believed in it and although I'd tease him about it, I never really said look it's a cop-out you know very well, because he didn't think it was. He believed he was close to the stars and close to the seasons. And looking back at the old days we had, and remembering the way he talked, I believe he was close to the stars and as far as I'm concerned he is always alive to the seasons and the stars when I come back from London or wherever I have been.

First thing, coming through Sapperton Tunnel, I see that old wall and I think, that's Frank, crumbling a bit, a refuge for sheep, standing there in the winds on the top of the hills, dry stone wall. That's Frank, indestructible.

Frank had this double loyalty or threefold loyalty. He went to the village school in Bisley. Miserden was also very much an alter ego as it was part of the triangle with the Salt Box down the road, and he was also very closely connected with Sheepscombe where we've got a seat for him looking out over the cricket field.

He was a demon bowler in the Sheepscombe side. He used to come up the hill, it was a sloping field, and you'd see the top of his head as he was running up, then you would see his shoulders, furious face, and then the rest of his body. It was just like a galleon coming over the horizon, all guns blazing, and he'd whip the ball down and if the ball did not kill the batsman, furious anger and frustration would kill him.

'That should a got thee,' he'd say. 'It should a got thee.' And if he didn't get five bloody heads in one innings he was a disappointed man, a terrorizer.

He was a Norman I think in many ways. I used to tease him about it:

'Frank Mansell,' I said, 'you came over, you were a predator, you were one of the conquerors who showed off, you were responsible.'

'Ah,' he said, 'that was in the old days, we had some land then, we lost it all, through bewilderment, and drink and corruption.'

'Not corrupt, not corruption Frank, you were never corrupt.'

You'll find the old Norman names very often amongst the villages. Frank half admitted that Frampton Mansell was part of his heritage and that his ancestors came from there, but he thought that they had lost it, that it had slipped through their hands, largely due to . . . Let me put it like this, hey loved too much, they drank too much, they lived too much and they never put anything by, except his honesty and his character. And that's why he ended up digging holes in the road for the post office, and writing this most marvellous poetry.

Which was the true voice of the Cotswolds. And I can hear him now, but I can't remember his style. There is a recording of us both giving a double recital, you can imagine the feeling, the daredevil feeling we had at Cheltenham Ladies' College. We marched in together, him on the left of stage and me on the right, and we really played to the audience:

'Any questions?'

'Yes, what makes you a true poet?'

'Never get married,' he said. 'Never get married, it's death to poetry.'

He was married twice as far as I know and gave people a lot of happiness, but in dropping that bombshell at Cheltenham Ladies' College, it made the teachers twitch a bit.

4

Bulls Cross

We're sitting on a seat at Bulls Cross which is the . . . I cannot give it its London equivalent, it would be improper to give it its London equivalent, because there isn't an equivalent. It's the meeting of all the roads from all the valleys around, from the Painswick Valley, the Stroud Valley, Bisley, Birdlip. The high road from Stroud to Birdlip comes through the beech wood, Frith wood, and runs just behind us.

That's the highway, going through the wood, the old highway from Stroud to Birdlip and then on from Birdlip to Oxford, to Cheltenham, Droitwich and the salt mines, and if you turn right it goes on to the Urals, where the wind blows from. There are branches off to Sheepscombe on the left, there is a cross road which runs to Painswick and on to Gloucester, and the other way up over to a place we call the scrubs which is just near Bisley. It also branches off and goes down King Charles Lane to Steanbridge farm and Steanbridge pond and continues up King Charles Lane.

The other lane running down here, the lower lane into Stroud, is called Wick Street. It's an alternative way into Painswick because Painswick used to be called Wick, meaning a dairy farm. Then the local warlord or mafia, Pain, he took it over and from then on – he was the lord of the manor, he said – he took it over and enclosed much of the land. And it has been ever since called Painswick. But we know it as Wick, because the street is called Wick and the street is older than he is. We don't stand any of that nonsense, any of that malarkey, although some of his relations, some of his descendants, still run some firms in Stroud, like estate agents, Davies Champion and Pain, or Smith Ball and Pain, they were cloth manufacturers and legal, they had us all sewn up long ago.

But I'm very interested in Wick Street. It has some marvellous old manor houses which you don't see on the Victorian Road, which is the upper one with all the traffic on it, the main road now. Wick Street, the old road to Painswick, has some superb manor houses. Painswick is architecturally splendid and it has a wonderful church. We used to say it has the third-best peel of bells in the country. And on certain nights we used to hear the peel in Slad when the wind was in the right direction. It is the most beautiful peel of bells. It's in that church where King Charles stabled some of his horses, when he was on his way back from Gloucester. We never forgave him. We didn't mind him being defeated; we were really on the side of the common man, although we've got a lot of royalty living around us. I'm not sure whose side they are on, living up on the high ground, I won't mention their names. One lives in Highgrove, one lives in Tetbury, one lives near Bisley. I think they are still retreating from Gloucester.

Then there is another high road that goes up to Bisley, Bisley Old Road, from Stroud. It goes right up to Bisley and then on to Cirencester. And then the third one, which goes up to Rodborough, Amberley, Minchinhampton, Cirencester and then onto London. This cross road from Gloucester to Painswick is here too. This is a Piccadilly Circus. Incidentally, all those little hollows in this common land, I think this is where King Charles's defeated army was buried. But a lot of it was stone that went to build the houses and the walls, the farmhouses and the farm walls.

I remember when I was young, when I was a kid, we always came up here to play if we didn't go to the pond. There was a young Vic, a Dorothy Vic, and a young boy Norman, one of the great families of farmers, and I went home and told my sister that they were sitting in one of these hollows. Dorothy was all blushing and showing the ring on her finger, looking at her finger and blushing, and her sisters were overwhelmed with excitement at such gossip. And of course he had just proposed to her, they were married the next year. They lived up on the top of the hill, a lovely old couple, both gone now. But one could see the hatching, the brood hatching, of this young pair.

I also used to meet a girlfriend from Gloucester who stayed with an aunt in Painswick and would come over. She used to meet me on the hill and we used to go into the wood and read Shakespeare together, *Macbeth*. She played Lady Macbeth until the middle of the play and then she discovered there was no other part for her, because Lady Macbeth disappears. So she took over my part. I was Macbeth but then I had to be Duncan. Women, they impose their own rules. She was older than me and went to a grammar school. I only went to the local school. So that was my first lesson in Shakespeare and also in female domination. But I still remember every word. I remember most of that play, through learning it in that beech wood.

There is an old stone milestone here, it's really worth looking at closely, because it's cut into steps where the old men used to get on their horses. The other milestone is in the wall of the village school, opposite The Woolpack, down in Slad. And there's one further milestone beyond the village, it still exists, it's been protected by time. Most of them have gone now.

It's on a corner where a sweep once lived. He had a van, a van full of soot. Once, going round the bend very fast on the wrong side of the road, the car turned over on him. It smothered him with soot and he choked to death. We still, happily, call it Sooty Corner. People round here would say, 'He was going round Sooty Corner, see.' Well just round Sooty Corner is the other milestone where I always stopped and kissed my knee when I was running to school, my secondary school, in Stroud. I'd always get a stitch coming down the hill towards Sooty Corner, I'd always get the stitch. You sat on the milestone and kissed your knee, it was supposed to cure your stitch. And then I would go into the second lap, get to school in 25 minutes, running. On the way back, the three miles would take two hours with Eileen Brown, discovering the landscape, and Rosie and Edna who went to the neighbouring girls' school. That's when education begins, as you walk out of that gate and sprawl over the landscape and discover just what the quality of this valley was and discover your own qualities.

And also if it was raining, or if girls like Eileen or Doreen weren't around, I used to slip into the Stroud public library for which I am still enormously grateful. They are talking of shutting down public libraries. But the amazing difference that it had to me was going on a cold night, for there was always heating on, there wasn't always heating at home.

I did all my early reading in Stroud library. I discovered people I had never heard of, like Joyce, Ezra Pound, D. H. Lawrence, Eliot. I remember finding Huxley's *Brave New World*. I borrowed it from the library and I was sitting by the war memorial in Slad reading it when the vicar came out of the vicarage. He saw me reading it and snatched it from me.

'That profane book! Ye who doth read profanities shall be destroyed by fire,' he said, 'and I quote.' But he didn't, though he sounded as though he were quoting some dramatic death sentence from the Bible. But he took the book away. I had to tell them at the library that the vicar had seized the book and destroyed it as being profane. And could they let me off the fine.

Well I thought I've touched something very sensitive here. So I'll follow up Huxley, so I read *Chrome Yellow*, and others. I did some immensely important reading there, but the particular quality of it that remains when I look back was that it was uninstructed reading. It was the public library that provided it, and still provides it.

But Lawrence and Joyce, who I got to know by heart, were probably the early influences, and I thought I had personally discovered them. I didn't know that anyone else knew about them. I'd gone along the shelves and I'd found these fascinating writers and I thought nobody else had ever heard of them. Youth, it's the time for learning. If I'd only had more time at school, without all those wasted hours on Sir Walter Scott. I'll never forgive Walter Scott. That heavy, cement, Latinized prose, a real pain that was. I'm told he gets on rather well now on television, they make drama, in starch new costumes. You can always tell when they are putting on a master new work on television, everybody suddenly comes out. Even out of the ditches, all the poverty-stricken miners come out with starched white shirts and special grime. I think the camera work is shot through some kind of gauze, meaning that this scene isn't now, these are Victorian days and everybody speaks in a special stagey Victorian accent.

I remember one chap, a decent chap, who was full of affection when he made *Cider with Rosie* about fifteen years ago. He put all the schoolgirls in . . . He put all the girls in white pinafores and all the boys were wearing brand new caps straight out of the wardrobe. Well, we were very poor and ragged and I thought that was a misjudgement so I said, 'Before you start, get all the boys to jump on their caps,' which they were all happy to do. They put them in the gutter and all whooped and jumped and got their caps into what I call a sense of realism, ragged and muddy, so they were all right. They don't always remember to pay the past its rightful claim, that we were a grubby lot. That was just part of the reality of life. We weren't filthy, we were grubby and unkempt. We'd wear a shirt for two days running and old neckties, you'd never see a creased shirt. There's a photograph of some of the lads and a horse and trap outside the Star Inn, just below The Woolpack. The landlord, it shows he's the landlord; he's very short, he's smoking a clay pipe and his trousers look as though they are made of stove piping. They haven't seen an iron, they haven't been creased for months, obviously, but that was the character of the day. And the old men used to wear straps, their trousers pulled up and straps just above the knee, or just below the knee sometimes, to keep their trousers out of the mud.

I'd like to see more recognition of what the past was really like, that it had a reality that was in many ways brave, and dignified.

Just behind me where the signpost is there was a gibbet. When the whole country was run for wool the various lords of the manor were very keen on stopping sheep-stealing, so they had a gibbet here, and they had a gibbet on the war memorial near the green in Sheepscombe. Now the hangman used to live down at Dead Combe Bottom, in a lane going down through the wood, deep into the valley. He had a cottage there. I remember it well. But the story that haunts the gibbet was that one night he was called out to string up a sheep-stealer. He came up, got the rope and took in charge a shivering lad. He put the noose round his neck and strung him up. It was a very stormy night but as the culprit was swinging and struggling and dying, the cloud was torn away from the moon by the gale and the moon shone on the face of this strangled young man and the hangman recognized the face of his son. He did not know until that moment that he was hanging his son. He went down, he said no more, he said nothing, he went down to his cottage in Dead Combe, and there was a hook. I remember going down there and you would go into the kitchen and there was a big iron hook on the wall and he went in there and he hung himself. And the house, the cottage, over the years, was never inhabited again; it just fell down brick by brick. And I can remember going in there in its state of decay, we used to play in there, not insensible to the mystery of it all, you know what kids are like, they like a bit of drama.

But that was a very haunting story to most of the villagers and Bulls Cross was a traffic zone even in those days, busy. There was a stagecoach and the horses went wild taking a stagecoach down to Stroud and they bolted across this empty space here, they bolted and the stagecoach turned over and all the passengers were killed. And it's said, Granny Trill said,

'If you are at Bulls Cross at night on New Year's night you'll hear the neighing of these horses and the shrieking of women passengers and the breaking up of the carriage. And if you hear that, you won't survive the New Year, your face will go green.' 'Yer what, gran?' 'Your face will go green and you'll die by drowning.' And we believed her. We never came up here on New Year's night. We could hear the sound of the horses neighing over the top of the hill. But we'd never come up here; maybe it still happens. So I give you warning.

5

The Violin on the Wall

'Did you learn to play the violin at school?' I asked.

No, not at school. A chap used to come round, he wasn't a teacher but he used to come round on a bicycle. He held violin classes in a room in a cottage up the road, I must have been eight or nine I think. We had to pay so much for lessons and we had to pay so much a week for the violin, though they were a bit rubbishy; they were Czechoslovakian, mass-produced. But once we'd paid for the violins he just disappeared. So we were left on our own. Some of us dropped out and the rest of us just taught ourselves. I remember a saying once, the trouble about a violin, it's a most marvellous instrument but you have to play for four or five years before anyone wants to listen to you.

When I got older and left the village I played for money in the streets. People used to drop a penny or two and then one time an old colonel said to me, 'Why aren't you at work young man?' and then he blushed and dropped in a sixpence in my bag to cover his confusion, because nobody was at work during those days. People were just wandering all over England, trying to find work. That's how I started but when I got to Worthing I played outside an old people's home and the porters were pushing, in wheelchairs, these very old pomaded women and I reckon until I was moved on by the police I made – they were paying me in two-shilling pieces, and I think I was playing 'Danny Boy' at the time, one of those and then a hymn tune or two – I made 38 shillings, which was twice the amount a man could make in a week in those days if you had a proper job. So I knew I was onto a good thing. And it kept me going and through a year in Spain I was able to live on it and come back with £10 into the bargain. But I didn't get that through playing the violin. There were other methods.

That was when I went to work in a hotel during the winter. I saved my tips. I used to work in the kitchen in the day and play in the saloon at night. I'd play the sort of stuff you used to get in the Palm Court in Bournemouth. I had a little German friend called Rudolpho and he played a squeezebox. I've still got one of the programmes. And the stuff we used to play: paso dobles, divertimentos, Mozart, Irving Berlin. We just gave it to them, all these old ladies sitting around, this was before the tourists had started to come. We had a captive audience with nothing to spend their money on but booze and us, with this great sea; the hotel was on the beach, with the sea splashing against the hotel windows in the winter. We'd go into some Wagner, 'The Ride of the Valkyries' or *The Flying Dutchman*, we used to stir 'em up. I've never enjoyed life so much as at that time.

Then we'd go off into a market with all the produce. All the people and their children used to come and gather round, step on your toes, and just gaze at you, because there wasn't wireless and there wasn't television, and a musical instrument was a treat. They did not have to work, there was no work, it was a sort of a fiesta, a holiday. We never got any money from them but the old ladies used to throw me biscuits from upstairs rooms. I could always live on it.

I suppose I was in my early teens when I realized the one thing that was important in village life was the weekly dance. I got a little band together called The Three Blind Mice.

I knew a couple of other chaps were interested in playing dance music of a very rudimentary kind. We filled in a gap because at that time in the dances in the various villages around, there were no discos and no electronic music to dance to; it was long before those days. And the dance music would be performed under a very strict guide by perhaps some local well-meaning spinster. And if you were dancing and you swung a girl off her feet this well-meaning spinster, Miss . . . I've forgotten her name now, she would ram the top of the piano down, lock it and go home. Well you can't do that when youth is having its fling. So what we decided to do, the three of us, the chap on the drums was the local beekeeper who used to make honey and mead up the valley, the chap on the piano was a brother-in-law I think, Harold, from Stroud, and me on the violin. We collared the market, because it was very important to have a free-for-all dance once a week, a penny dance, not particularly sinful.

We got a chap who loved going out at night, he drove a little taxi and he loved getting away from home. There was no television so there was no reason why he should stay at home. He was a non-alcoholic. In order to get out of his house, he used to come and pick us up once a week and take us, free, to Bisley, Birdlip, Sheepscombe, Painswick, Slad of course, Ruscombe, Chalford. We were coining it. We were paid five shillings a dance and free lemonade. We were rich and not only that, we were able to transmit early jazz which we learned. The beekeeper had a lot of old jazz records and we could learn it from those.

Why we called ourselves The Three Blind Mice? Because none of us at that stage could read music. But we did very well.

The music we played was old-fashioned, most of it, all by ear, it could have been well-known foxtrots, or something you had learned from the cinema. Then some very odd dances. A type of barn dance, I can hear it now, though I don't know how to dance it. The Hesitation Dip was another one, perhaps you'd hear it on *Come Dancing*. The Hesitation Dip, very formal, Roger de Coverley was another one which was up the sides and down the middle. But generally speaking the foxtrots and rhumbas. I remember a girl in Painswick coming up and saying, 'Laurie, you're driving me crazy.' I thought, I've made it, I'm the Mick Jagger of the district. Then I realized she wanted a tune called 'You're Driving Me Crazy', which I can still hear now. It was a great disappointment . . . but only one of many.

I moved on later to grander things, out at Painswick. We had a larger band called The Painswick Orpheans, based on the Savoy Orpheans, and we used to play at the Institute there. We wore black ties and white shirts that only came down to one's middle. It was a con actually. They were actually made of paper, or something very like that, if you can imagine; disposable dinner jackets, or dinner shirts, that's what they were. But we reached a zenith of importance; we were the only ones providing dance music in the whole of the area. Boys and girls used to come on their bikes from miles around. We had a saxophone, trumpet, violin, piano, drums, though not a guitar, this was before guitars came sweeping in from Europe. And one or two radiantly attractive 'groupies'. We'd made it, we had power. In all of our little area, there was no one to compete with us. We had the power that now follows the rock bands of today. We had it yesterday.

Power, sexual power, that comes from leading a dance band. I tasted in those days such a sense of glory, of fame. Then the Beatles arrived and my life was finished. I had to take up classical music instead, which, seriously, has been the great consolation of my life. Jazz, I discovered Ellington when I was about twelve or thirteen, Duke Ellington and Satchmo, Fats Domino and the rest of them, I used to save up to buy their records and as you know, they were the great prophets of jazz, the classicists of jazz, 'Mood Indigo' and 'Creole Rhapsody'. My mother didn't like that and made me go and play them out in the privy, that's when I had a wind-up gramophone.

Before then, not having a gramophone, when I was keen on learning and extending my knowledge of classical music, I used to buy from Stroud for about three shillings these little seven-inch records, Schubert and Brahms. But there was nowhere to play them. So I used to take them in a carrier bag and bicycle in the rain right up to Birdlip where I had friends, in order to put on this record, which they did not want me to play, but they were very kind. I'd play it and then bicycle all the way home.

To think in those days music was such a unique treasure, and had to be suffered for. Now it's everywhere around you, you can't get away from it. Music is on the walls, on the floors, in the pubs, supermarkets. Music in those days was a sought-for experience. And I think it made it more appreciated.

I first learned to play the violin as a young child at home. In the kitchen there was a violin hanging on the wall, it always intrigued me, this shape. I didn't really know what it was to begin with, it was one of the first symbols of exotic interest. You had bed warmers in those days and you had pictures of the family hanging on the wall but this shape fascinated me. I asked my mother what it was and she said, 'It belongs to your father.' Well, dad had already left home, left us and gone, but it belonged to him. And she said, 'You play it, it's a musical instrument.' So I got it down and we dusted it up and we got it into running order, and that's when this chap used to come round giving lessons. Instead of buying the Czechoslovakian mass-produced one, I had this one. It was a copy of a 'Strad', it had a wonderful tone. I kept this first violin for years, I took it to Spain with me. It got crushed by a passing bull in Malaga. It was partly that, partly the heat, the heat melted the gum, but I like to say it was crushed by a passing bull who had a very bad ear for music.

And I thought, I've come to the end now, I'm not going to be able to live. But just at that time I met a German student who'd fallen in love with a Spanish girl and they were going to run away together and they had to travel light. And he said:

'Oh, by the way, do you want a violin? I've got one and I can't be bothered with all this stuff. We're going over the sierras tomorrow.'

'Yes,' I said, 'funny you should say that.'

'Come round tonight and we'll meet in the tavern and you can have it. I'll be glad to get rid of it.'

So I moved into that one and it was even better than my imitation Stradivarius. And that's the one I've got now.

And from then on when I got back to England I played seriously. But having no sense of coordination I can only play one note at a time. I can play the Women's Institute recorder, no trouble at all, but I can't play a piano because I can't do with my left hand something that is separate from my right hand. But the violin was made for me. It's portable and I can follow the line with my left hand on the strings and by this time I could read music, and I discovered other musicians, pianists, cellists, and we moved into this world of cosmic music, I'm going to be pompous now, but it is a world starting in Gloucestershire. I only realized when I got back here that this was a country of memorable composers: Elgar and Gustav Holst, Vaughan Williams. I was going to say Rimsky-Korsakov but he was only here as a refugee briefly and he didn't like the country, it wasn't cold enough for him. But there was a local tradition for music and I moved on with great satisfaction.

You can go anywhere in Ireland because there is a tradition of playing the violin, Irish reels and laments.

They play on their own and you can go round the country on your own. That's what I always hoped, that one day I might tour Ireland with my violin, because you don't need any accompaniment and you are always welcome.

These days I cannot play, I cannot see the strings, they are almost breaking up. I cannot play 'Killarney', there is too much jumping around, I can play 'Early One Morning'. I can play 'Abide With Me'.

The only thing left now with my eyes going is music. I can't read. Music is my constant companion, especially Beethoven, Bach. How lucky I am.

My brother was older than me, he was what is known as a fixer. He was always getting out of things. He never ran errands, he always went and hid in the grass when mother was asking us to go and borrow a screw of tea from Miss Turk up the road, he'd never be visible. We got rid of him, we sent him to Australia. We had a collection and bought him a single ticket to Australia where I think he's doing very well. I get a postcard with sheep from him occasionally.

Mother got him a violin because he had to do what I was doing. He went to the classes later on, but there was only one bow, which came with his violin. Father's violin didn't have a bow. So I found in my school music teacher's report, it says, 'Lack of bow has spoilt his chances, but think he will do well.' I used to go in there, brother Jack having the bow, and, may I say, little talent – Jack are you listening, I'm paying off some old scores now. He had the bow and the violin and I had the violin and no bow. So I had to spend weeks and weeks going through just left hand and just waving the right hand about.

I learnt the violin in a class in a cottage up the road but here in this schoolroom, this lovely long room, is where I held my first public performance, which was a raging success. I was playing with Miss Eileen Brown. In the parish magazine I remember the headline:

'Violin and piano duet with Miss Eileen Brown and young Laurie Lee.'

And we were playing, well we hoped we were playing 'The Poet and Peasant Overture', but it wouldn't stay on the music stand, it kept falling on the floor. So I hissed to her, 'Give 'em "Danny Boy"', so as a back-up we played 'Danny Boy'. We didn't know how it was going to go, we weren't very sure, then suddenly we got together and we played. We found, as it were, a meeting place halfway through the tune and it then flowed like honey and the whole audience, the old women, my mother, my sisters, they all began to sing in chorus with us. And that was it, because until then they'd just been fidgeting. But then they began to sing with us. But not only were they paying us this great compliment of accompanying us; we'd stirred this ancestral memory in them, but they were using their hymn-singing voices which was the great compliment. It showed how seriously they were taking it, tears running down their faces, down my mother's face and Eileen's mother's face, running down my sisters' faces too, sister Marge bless her. I like the thought it was emotion but, well it could have been, could have been. But I think they were tears of laughter.

6

The Village School

This, my first school, was a school for four-year-olds to twelve-year-olds. I remember the windows looking out onto the valley. We were half prisoners and also half special on a special platform, to be able to see the valley and everything that was happening.

The far end of the room was just called 'the infants'. The young four-year-olds, five-year-olds used to come in through a little door at the end, that was their entrance. The 'big 'uns' from seven or eight onwards used to come in through a door at the other end of the room, and they didn't meet. And then you had this great occasion when you were filtered through from the infants to the other end of the room when you had to start a new system of education and behaviour. It was a great day. It was a great day. I think my brother Jack was the only one who didn't go through the two stages because he was a genius you see. He used to flash away all day like a pin table and bully the teachers in that high bullying tone he had developed from quite early on.

The walls were covered with maps the colour of tea. There was a wall of maps with all the colonial possessions marked in red and we used to sit there; we were very poor in those days, poor but uncomplaining, we lived on boiled and baked cabbage, the poorest of the poor. And we used to sit there and look at this world map and think, looking at these maps and thinking, we are the greatest in the world. We own all those pieces of red on that map, on that world map. The whole of Africa, the whole of India, all those islands across the Pacific. Then we'd look at each other as if we were centurions, as we were, politically, in those days. We were the Roman occupiers, except that we were the serfs, we didn't know that, but we were.

So I learnt that but particularly I'm grateful for being introduced to some of the old country songs, here in this room and some of the longer poems of Milton and Shakespeare which I wouldn't have known otherwise. I wouldn't have known them from the library, because I wouldn't have known where to find them. So I have only the deepest gratitude for these various stepping stones of education.

But to be set in this special valley was to learn both sides of the world. And this school, there would have been forty kids in it, from right up the end of the valley down to the Vatch,* and that's how we learned about our community and now, stumbling round Stroud, these gnomes, looking very like me, will come up and say, 'Hello Laurie', and I know he was at school with me. And we were at school here and we enjoyed that same privilege, hard times but invaluable, irrecoverable and never to be forgotten.

In this room, in this village school, I learnt early poetry. There were two rather waspish teachers who didn't think much of me, especially Miss Wardley, the headmistress. I used to go home to dinner, it was just up the road, I had baked cabbage or something and it's still a habit of mine after lunch, or dinner as we called it, to drop into a heavy sleep, like an animal on safari. And she would come round with a ruler and poke me and say, 'Wake up you, you with your little red eyes.' And I thought, that's no way to talk to a sensitive youth, but that's how she is. Then I also had a steady sniff and she used to say, 'Laurie Lee, will you

* A farm cottage between Slad and Stroud.

please go outside and blow your nose and don't come back in until you're clear.' And I used to go outside seething with rage, thinking, I'm really a prince, she doesn't know that and one day, when I come into my throne, when I come into my kingdom, I'll see to her. I won't be too unkind, I'll just lock her up for a few decades. Eventually when I had got that indignation off my chest I'd come back in and she'd say, with a freezing smile, 'A little less beastly now I hope.'

But on the other hand, Miss Wardley, who used to wear glass jewellery that would swing and tinkle as she walked, she introduced us to poetry and I know yards of poetry, thanks to her and her assistant teacher. What a wonderful age it is, to be in that age, not being bombarded by television, jukeboxes, or the wireless, to have it straight off the page at the age when you are at your most absorbing. I can to the point of boredom tell you the whole of 'Il Penseroso' by Milton, learned when I was about eight. Don't encourage me because it goes on for about three pages. And some of the country songs like 'Down in the Valley' and 'Early One Morning', that still means this valley to me:

> Early one morning, just as the sun was
>   rising,
> I heard a maiden sing in the valley below,

Oh! don't deceive me, oh never leave me,
How could you use such a poor maiden so?

I've carried that around as an amulet of conscience ever since I learnt it here, and anyone who says I have a casual attitude to women is lying in their feminist teeth.

When I came back from mooning round the world, just after I had published *Cider with Rosie*, I came back to the village. My school, the village school, was still there – but the local council wanted to close it down and I wrote to the Minister of Education and said this is a community, this is where we began. This is where the children get to know both the valley and themselves. They don't just get to know the inside of a bus. They're here. And he reprieved it. A dastardly thing then happened and I'm not going to be . . . I'm going to be frank about this. It was a trick of outrageous insensitivity. The year, the month, that Aberfan school was destroyed by the coal tip that plunged down the hillside and buried Aberfan school and half its schoolchildren, the council wrote to all the parents in this district saying: 'your village school is in imminent peril of destruction by landslide, we cannot guarantee that your children will be safe for more than two weeks'.

This school is built on rock as are all the other houses up and down the valley, and we said, 'It won't be destroyed in two weeks, it won't be destroyed in twenty years.' But the parents had to believe what they heard. The council said that the surveyor had condemned it, but it was merely a way of closing the school. I thought then that it was an outrageously dirty trick and still do. And may the Gloucestershire County Education blush with shame if they hear me say it. I expect they have all gone now anyway.

7

The Woolpack

'We're not working out a soap opera, we're living our own particular history.'

The Woolpack's my local. It's a very old pub. It used to be, as its name suggests, a place where the pack horses from the hills, bringing the wool down to Stroud, to the Stroud mills, used to stop here for refreshment, the mules and other horses were also refreshed. Then, when the new road came in, The Woolpack, bless its heart, suddenly sprang in height so it's now about four storeys when it used to be just a little hovel on the old road behind where we are sitting. But it is none the less elegant for that. It's got great character as you can see.

There were a number of other pubs around where those who were bringing the wool down, mule trains, would stop and have a refresher. So you get The Fleece, and The New Fleece, there's a Woolpack in Stonehouse, there are two Fleeces in Stroud. And apart from those we've got a few royal pubs, which obliquely refer to the defeat of Charles I who got thumped in the siege of Gloucester and who went from Bisley down what we now call King Charles Lane. There's a pub in Painswick called The Royal Oak. In a way, we named it after this defeated royal out of a kind of pity, an affectionate pity, I think. We've got a lot of retreating royals round here, up in the hills, at least four. I'd better mention no names or bang goes my knighthood. But they're all retreating. We're fond of them as long as they keep their place up the oak tree. Prince Charles, I'll meet him in The Royal Oak in Painswick, if they'll let him in.

The Woolpack is on the old, lower lane running through Slad, on the lane where I have a cottage. This lower lane used to be the main road. It comes past the Elizabethan house called the Old House. In the Victorian period, about the mid-1800s, they built a new road from Stroud to Bulls Cross and up to Birdlip and that road was raised above the level of the old road. Now I swear, and most of the villagers agree with me, that The Woolpack was one floor lower, facing the old lane. When they put the new road in, quite obviously, for business, they raised it a floor or two to face the new road. But dear old David* won't have it, he says: 'This is the oldest building in Slad, you can just tap the walls and you'll find it's the old stone. It's the original Woolpack.' It's not the original prices, but never mind, he's welcome to his own opinion, but only just.

Structurally, it looks such an odd building, like a skyscraper almost. It was a nice piece of re-design when the new road came through. And if you go up the new road now, you'll find that the church and the village school are both built around 1830. Nothing is older than that. Go along the old lane and all the cottages are 1600. So I fear David and I have an argument so far as The Woolpack is concerned.

The Woolpack hasn't been changed much since then. The landlords who come here get transfixed with the atmosphere and they stay for life. I don't suppose you'll see the end of David now until he takes one of his boats and slides away on the immortal launch and goes seven times round the world in the wrong direction, and then he'll turn up again. But at the moment this bar and the next bar are architecturally unchanged, and this is very rare

* The then landlord.

for a village pub because they are usually got at by developers, by the brewers, by others. So we are very at home here. I remember it with such vividness because the central bar, where Martin is sitting – Martin's the man with the beard looking like Karl Marx, a good lad – that was the scene of a famous occasion when I was a boy. Vincent, an ex-village lad, had broken two taboos. One taboo, he'd left the village, which you are not supposed to do as a young man, you stick with the village through thick and thin. He'd left the village and gone abroad, gone to New Zealand. But worse than that, he broke a second taboo. He came back, loaded with gold and boasting.

And he dropped in here just before Christmas one snowy night, flashing his gold coins around. He said not only how rich he was and that he ate meat every day, and that he never touched his cap to anyone.

'Not like you, grovelling on the mud of Stroud. All you see of society is Stroud on a Saturday night. Me I have a horse and carriage at home in New Zealand and I eat meat every day, and what's more, I pay for my drinks in gold.' And he brought out these sovereigns and he laid them out on the counter. And he kept on ordering drinks and flashing his gold around and the young men sitting round watched him, they drank his drink, they kept silent, but they kept watching him, quiet eyes and glowing cigarettes, which he bought for them. Then one by one they slipped away into the blizzard. He went on until closing time, then he paid for his bill and went out into the snow and walked up to where his parents lived at the top of the village. He walked up singing into the blizzard. I'm sure I heard him singing that night. People in the village could hear that boasting, singing voice going up.

But as he got near the war memorial the lads met him, and stopped him and said, 'Well, Vincent,' and they hit him and they knocked him down and they kicked him. They stole his watch and they threw him over the wall. And in the morning he was found frozen to death.

You don't go away, and you don't come back boasting of riches which the young men had not been able to achieve. If you come back a pauper, on your hands and knees asking for soup, they'll take you in and look after you. But if you come back throwing your gold sovereigns down on the bar, flashing your gold watches, they don't forgive that. He wasn't exactly murdered, he was ritually slaughtered. We clammed up and we were told as children never to mention it. Later, about ten years later, an old woman, the mother of one of those who'd killed him, was dying. She saw a stranger sitting by her bed and she said, 'Who's this?' And her daughter said, 'Don't worry, it's only a police gentleman, he doesn't want to make any trouble he just wants to know what happened to the watch, mother, that's all he wants to know.'

And the old lady sat up in bed and looked at him, then laid back, closed her eyes, and died.

I like to feel that's how we guarded ourselves in the past. Nobody ever spoke, nobody ever went to the police, but we all knew 'who done it'. And Vincent's murderers grew to be respectable parishioners, parents, but they treated Vincent . . . well, he was a vagabond. All this happened in this pub, the place in which judgement was passed.

Many other happier things have happened in here. We have harvest festivals here, when you cannot move for blotched cauliflowers and magnificent vegetable marrows, free drinks and the vicar going slowly green on cider, which he's not normally accustomed to. It's a great night, the harvest festival.

And it's also a great place for refreshment and relaxation. I can lean out of the window and watch who calls to my cottage. I can see the turn of the road and see the three ashen. There used to be three ash trees, they've gone, but we still call it the three ashen. I can see the arrivals and departures of strangers and the arrivals we hope for. Of new loves and new engagements, new pleasures and the departures of visitors from Bristol, hoping they will return. From this angle you can see the rain coming up from Wales. It comes round the corner in a silver sheet, just in time for you to get down into the house, take in your washing, stay in for the night or stay here for the night.

You can see Peter Webb, the farmer. You can see his fields which are laid out in almost an Elizabethan lozenge, I don't think the hedges have been changed since Elizabethan days; certainly his farm is that old. And we know when if he cuts his hay before five o'clock, by eleven it's raining. We say, 'Peter's cut his hay, we'd better take cover.' Peter keeps our sense of the seasons alive watching his fields, we know what time of the year it is. And he's a very correct and accomplished farmer, he's been there for fifty years. And I still know his voice, calling his cows, calling his sheep. His is the voice of the valley and the voice of the landscape. So I'm devoted to old Peter. Even if he does cut his hay in the rain, he knows what he's doing.

*

I think it's true that you should never return. I've been forgiven. I returned at a difficult time because, unlike Vincent who hadn't told a lot of stories about the village, I had. And you can tell any story in the bar about your neighbours and it's a joke, but you put it in print and you've broken a taboo. It took me a lot of time, living that down. But if you live in a village there is this tight enclosed community. We're not working out a soap opera, we're living our own particular history, and sharing that particular history of failures, disasters, happiness, life and death, marriages. But at least it's shared. And each of us thinks at times we are isolated. That we know the secrets of everybody else, but think that we ourselves are protected by isolation. We're not. We know the secrets of everyone else, thank God at the expense of their knowing our secrets too. And this is something that one must admit and acknowledge and be glad of. That to share the life of a community, you have to be part of a community, you can't watch it from a distance, you have to be involved in it, as they are involved in you.

As a writer, I would say that whether or not putting it all down on paper sets you apart from the community depends on how you tell the stories of the village. I wrote a bit about an uncle who I adored, he was one of the heroes of my youth. He drove a bus, a double-decker bus, and he liked cider, and he'd stand no nonsense. He once got out of his bus when we were coming back from Weston on an outing. There was a man in a hedge threatening his wife. My uncle stopped the bus, got out and knocked the man through the hedge, in order to protect the wife. Then the wife attacked him for having hit her husband. But he gets back into the bus and drives home singing. And we all think top Uncle Sid, because he was a hero.

But he got into trouble. He got his double-decker bus stuck under a railway bridge and we as boys went to see what had happened and he'd been sacked. He'd been sacked because he'd got a jar of cider in the front of his bus, and I mentioned this quite naturally. His children thought it was a bit excessive, abominable in fact, to tell these stories about Uncle Sid, in print. The *Evening Standard*, the London *Evening Standard* did some excerpts and they used that excerpt, so I wrote to, no I telephoned, my cousin and I said I was very sorry and I wasn't thinking, 'I do apologize and I'll cut it out of the next edition.' 'Oh you don't have to do that, there's no occasion to do that you know,' she said. She was obviously being very kind to me but I do understand that he is part of the book, therefore I wish it to be known what a hero he was and why he was such a hero to me and it did go into print. It was meant as a tribute of my affection for him, and my admiration for him, and so it's still there.

I must end up by saying when my book *Cider with Rosie* came out I thought I'll have a go, and I wrote to local cider makers and suggested because they would get a certain amount of publicity for their product, they might send me a crate or two. 'Oh no, we don't have anything to do with the scandal you've caused in your village by having an affair with an under-age girl.' I'm hoping that one day they'll bring this up again in the committee meeting and perhaps be a little more tolerant to the fact that I was used. I wasn't a predator. I was used and they may still send me round a crate.

I was sitting outside the pub recently and two girls came up to me. They were part of a school group, it was about five to eleven. They were doing 'O' levels and they said to me, 'Excuse me sir, can you tell me where Laurie Lee's buried?' A certain shiver of mortality ran through me and I said, 'He's in the public bar, otherwise he'd be up in the woods.'

*

Towards the end of the last century a local artist did a series of lithographs based on churches of various villages: Bisley, Sheepscombe, Painswick, Ranwick and Slad, of all places. Before he embarked on these he got a list of subscribers and it was based on selling his lithographs to the gentry and the high ones and the moral ones and the grandees. So when he did Slad, you'll notice when you are just coming into the village, there's the school there and the church there. It's a very romantic little lithograph, I love it. There's one of my ancestors sitting on the wall as you'll see, in a long bucolic gown.

But if you search very deeply into that picture, you won't find The Woolpack, because what he'd done was to remove The Woolpack deliberately, so that the patrons would not be offended by having the pub obscure the church. That's why you can suddenly see this view of Slad which doesn't exist otherwise. In fact, it's been censored, it's been de-alcoholized and that's why I love it. I always pretend the bucolic figure on the wall is me, but it obviously isn't. But I have got that gown still.

8

Home

When I was working in London towards the end of the war, a thistledown blew past my window and the movement of this thistledown brought me back here.

'Thistle, blue bunch of daggers, rattling upon the wind.'

That was the field, the church field just below the village.

And the poem 'Summer Rain', it's the same.

I hear the sad rinsing of reeded meadows
The small lakes rise to the wild, white rose
The shudder of wings in the streaming
  cedars
And tears of lime running down from the
  hills.

That sums up, those two verses sum up, all round here. The cedars in the garden of that big house and the streams running down through the limestone hills:

> And I hear the sad rinsing of reeded meadows

. . . because the rain would never stop. It was one of those summers:

> And the small lakes rise to the wild, white rose

Imagine, it's been happening just this week when the white roses are just opening and then the rain batters them, collects in them and flattens them. It's a disappointed summer. It's a summer that's been laid and written off, a summer that cannot be regained.

I wrote a lot of poetry that marked the changing seasons.

Apples

Behold the apples' rounded world
juice-green of July rain,
the black polestar of flowers, the rind
mapped with its crimson stain.

The russet, crab and cottage red
burn to the sun's hot brass,
then drop like sweat from every branch
and bubble in the grass.

They lie as wanton as they fall,
and where they fall and break,
the stallion clamps his crunching jaws,
the starling stabs his beak.

In each blunt gourd the cidery bite
of boys' teeth tears the skin;
the waltzing wasp consumes his share,
the bent worm enters in.

And I, with easy hunger, take
entire, my season's dole;
and welcome the ripe, the sweet, the sour
the hollow and the whole.

'Field of Autumn' I wrote here in Slad. It's the end of summer and I had a certain amount of difficulty finishing it. For instance, in the last verse when I say, 'Slow moves the hour that sucks our life', then, 'slow drops the late wasp from the flower'. But you don't have wasps dropping from flowers, it had to be a pear. It was about the disintegration of the year and the year's ripeness. Then I was trying to search for the finality of summer:

> The rose tree's thread of scent draws thin
> And snaps upon the air.

Which is, of course, a little death, when breath begins and breath ends. The rose tree's scent suddenly ends, finishes, there is no flower:

Field of Autumn

Slow moves the acid breath of noon
over the copper-coated hill,
slow from the wild crab's bearded breast
the palsied apples fall.

Like coloured smoke the day hangs fire
taking the village without sound;
the vulture-headed sun lies low
chained to the violet ground.

The horse upon the rocky height
takes all the valley in his eye,

yet dares not raise his foot or move
his shoulder from the fly.

The sheep snail-backed against the wall,
lifts her blind face but does not know
the cry her blackened tongue gives forth
is the first bleat of snow.

Each bird and stone, each roof and well,
feels the gold foot of autumn pass;
each spider binds, with glittering snare
the splintered bones of grass.

Slow moves the hour that sucks our life,
slow drops the late wasp from the pear,
the rose tree's thread of scent draws thin –
and snaps upon the air.

I was thinking of a poem today and I was going over it with my daughter. It was called 'At Night' and I haven't said it and I haven't remembered it since I first wrote it as a teenager, first in love. And it was a poem that was so obsessed by the touch of the images of love that it wrote itself without work:

At Night

I think at night my hands are mad,
for they follow the irritant texture of
  darkness
continually carving the sad leaf of your
  mouth
in the thick black bark of sleep.

And my finger-joints are quick with
  insanity,
springing with lost amazement
through a vast waste of dreams
and forming frames of desire
around the thought of your eyes.

By day the print of your body
is like a stroke of sun on your hands,
and the choir of your blood
goes chanting incessantly
through the echoing channels of my
  wrists.

But I am lost in my hut
when the stars are out,
for my palms have a catlike faculty of sight,

and the surface of every minute
is a swinging image of you.

Some poems require a certain amount of attention and rewriting, balancing of rhythms and images, but quite often they write themselves and you never touch them again. You don't need to. They're given to you. They've said what you wish to say. And this one I was looking at, I suppose I must have been about twenty years old, twenty-one, I still think it says what I wished to say at that time, so it doesn't require any more words.

Whereas in 'Field of Autumn', ending of summer required a way of saying it conclusively. I think the last lines and the last verses of poems are important, meaning that the conclusions should sum up what the rest of the poetry has said. It must end properly, it must end conclusively. It should not end in a mess or a squabble. Like a love affair, it should end correctly, creatively, with appreciation and celebration and forgiveness.

'Day of These Days' was dreamed up on a bright autumn morning on the top of a 14 bus going from the Fulham Road to the Strand. I had a job up there at the time and it was such a gold and glorious morning that the images of the morning began pouring into the top deck. So I was seeing the geraniums and the girls and golden light, and I began:

Such a morning it is when love
leans in through the geranium windows
and calls with a cockerel's tongue

And the old bus was ploughing along and I went through this various succession of verses summing up my feeling of autumn, most of them based on this valley and not on the Fulham Road. And I went on:

When the partridge draws back his string
and shoots like a buzzing arrow
over grained and mahogany fields.

And the images of that kind arranged themselves in succession ending up with:

Such a morning it is when all things
  smell good,
and the cheeks of girls
are as baked bread to the mouth

As bread and bean flowers
the touch of their lips

and their white teeth sweeter than
 cucumbers.

'Yates's bar!' yells the conductor and I was there, I was finished, the poem was over and I had got to Yates's bar. He knew where I was going because I used to go there every morning to get my supply of Portuguese periquito wine, which I used to work with. So there was the poem, ready written in the time that journey took. And the ticket, I remember it cost threepence, from the Fulham Road to Yates's bar in the Strand. And I was thinking the other day, you couldn't write a poem like that for threepence these days. It would cost you at least £1.90 perhaps. So that's where that was written and I still have some of the empty bottles. But something more serious than that. It was a game and a celebration of the gold side of autumn. But at the same time, I say it didn't require any rewriting, it made itself, and fitted into that bus ride:

Day of These Days

Such a morning it is when love
leans in through the geranium windows
and calls with a cockerel's tongue

And the partridge draws back his string
and shoots like a buzzing arrow
over grained and mahogany fields

When the mice
run whispering from the church
dragging dropped ears of harvest

And such a day it is when time
piles up the hills like pumpkins,
and the streams run golden

When all men smell good,
and the cheeks of girls
are as baked bread to the mouth

As bread and bean flowers
the touch of their lips
and their white teeth sweeter than
cucumbers.

Now you may say, it's a pity the bus ride wasn't further, giving you a chance to correct a few more of the verses. A bit slapdash but it's still a poem I enjoy. I enjoy repeating it. In the old days it gave me a kind of feeling of *joie de vivre*.

*

I wrote 'Moss Rose' in memory of my mother. But I can't remember it, I wrote it very briefly, very quickly, after she died, and I remember thinking of her, in terms I'd written about her in an early book of mine. She had this wonderful touch with flowers and I think it was largely a tribute to her, not only a memory but her touch in growing roses, moss roses, wild roses.

The BBC commissioned a number of poets to write poems which in some way reflected the bitterness of winter and the bitterness of the winter of war. And I couldn't get started on this poem. I said I would do one, then I didn't deliver anything and they enclosed a cheque and said when can we have the poem, the programme goes out on Friday. And on the Tuesday they rang up and asked if it was ready and I said yes. They said how long is it and I said it's about that long. I hadn't started it. Well we must have it on Thursday, so I said all right you'll have it by then. So on Wednesday night I started and I spent the whole of the evening writing about robins, I just couldn't get started. Then, about midnight, some lines came into my head about how bitter that winter was and the lines came in from nowhere, because before then I'd been messing about with these Woolworths images of Christmas cards.

It may not be a great poem but the lines were real and it goes:

Christmas Landscape

Tonight the wind gnaws
with teeth of glass,
the jackdaw shivers
in caged branches of iron,
the stars have talons.

There is hunger in the mouth
of vole and badger,
silver agonies of breath
in the nostril of the fox,
ice on the rabbit's paw.

Tonight has no moon,
no food for the pilgrim;
the rose tree is bare
and the ground is bitter with stones.

And this poem goes on for about twelve verses, this is just the beginning. When I'd got down the first verses, I thought I'm on a track now, that's the poem I wanted to write, so I put it away, got up before breakfast, finished it off and sent it to the BBC, and I've never changed it since. But I had to start it and I had to feel that the messages were coming through, that the images were floating in from Gloucestershire, and at that time I recognized them as true messages of the bitter winter of the war.

It was no good messing about with robins any more, I chopped up the robins and sent them to a bird fancier of mine. The power of 'the jackdaw shivers in caged branches of iron', 'the stars have talons', 'there is hunger in the mouth of vole and badger', 'silver agonies of breath in the nostril of the fox', 'ice on the rabbit's paw'.

I could go on, but that's the church bell ringing and the pub opens at seven.

9

Swift's Hill

I'm sitting at the foot of Swift's Hill. It seems to command the whole of the valley from Stroud up to Bulls Cross. Swift's Hill just stands here like a great ancestral hump. There are quarries here, partly limestone quarries, partly the old ragstone quarries. The old quarry man in Elcombe, I remember him well in a corner under the woods, he'd come to the quarries in the morning, he'd take out the stone and he built all the walls going down to Stroud. He was the last of the dry stone wall quarry men and this lovely old yellow stone comes from these quarries.

And behind me is Slad, my little village in the valley itself, it's one of a family of valleys. There's Sheepscombe, Painswick, Bisley, Chalford. They all have a kind of family likeness; same feel, same light, same trees, same families.

I think sometimes, I was brought up here, I was born here and I'm still living here, and I feel I know every detail of all this countryside around. And it's not only the trees and the stones and the houses, it's the people. They are all equally endemic, they are all rooted to this part. They are just as rooted to these parts as are the stones and the quarries and they have these family names like Swain, Partridge, Hogg, Webb, West, Lee, White, Fuller. A number of the names belong to the wool trade, Fuller for instance, Webb, Spinner. So when I think of this place it's not only for its undying, rapturous beauty, it turns slowly to the seasons and becomes a different person, equally beautiful, from spring to winter. But the people are the same. They are rooted. They are the valley, they are the Cotswolds. They don't move and they teach me their irreplaceability and I've learned that I don't move either. I come back and here I stay.

I've long wanted to know how to describe this part. I've long wished to discover a way of describing this part and the sensation of living here and associating the valley with the people and with its community and with its history; its pre-Roman, its pre-Bronze Age, its Stone Age history, and I suppose in a way it's been my life trying to filter through, in as simple a way as possible, a communication, a description, a condensation, a concentration of simple language, which can convey to others, not necessarily living in these parts, but living in other parts of Britain, what it's like to live here and what it's like to maintain this ancestral life. And a sense that I have of witnessing a moment in time which is reflected from the trees, from the quarried stone from the walls, from the houses, from the bleating animals who pass. The bleating sheep which you hear in the background who are passing on their ancestral fates, from one season to another.

I was sitting the other night in my garden, listening to the sheep, and I hope they'll forgive my saying so but it's the only time I've heard a sheep, a ewe, bleating with any kind of authority. Generally speaking they're wimps but when they have their lambs in the spring they suddenly take on a different kind of voice. Which the Hoggs do and the Webbs do when they grow and marry, they take on this same kind of authority, and I think the animals and the birds and the people do reflect the uniqueness of this valley. The blackbirds in my garden and the blackbirds in the garden at the end of the lane, they go off to Africa, as I did when I went around the world once as a young man, but they always come back here, they come back to the same garden, to the same tree, the same wall, the same nest and they imitate their ancestral voices, and no wonder they sing with a Gloucestershire accent because that's how they were raised.

When I went to London for the first time, people used to say:

'Why do you talk in that extraordinary American accent?'

'That's not American, that's Gloucestershire. We sailed from Bristol, we sailed from Plymouth, we were a West Country accent.'

'Oh, is that it? I thought you were Irish!'

These are green pods of valleys, they have a family shape. If you were dropped down into one of these valleys you would not know which one you were in because they are so alike in their verdant greenness. They're like pods. I was trying to describe it once to friends who didn't know this part, and I said that living in our valley was like being broad beans in a pod, so snug and enclosed and protective. And these valleys are just like that, they have this protective, miniature closeness, which in some ways explains why a lot of people still living in the village have never been to London, never even been to Swindon.

I tried to describe this valley through the seasons and how it changed, its personality changed, its character changed, so that in spring and summer and autumn and winter it was a different place, a different country almost and we boys, as kids, we were all ready to change our own attitude, our own games. It was either skating or it was snowballing or it was climbing trees, scragging apples. Whatever was true to that particular season was something we were ready to adapt ourselves to.

I remember walking through the village one very hard winter's morning, the dogs going by wrapped in the vapour of their breath and the boys not knowing quite what to do, they themselves wrapped in moist scarves, choking and pink faced. One said, 'What we goin' do then, eh?' Nobody knew what they were going to do and someone was flapping their arms and then another one, suddenly he took off and he began to whip himself with a stick. 'Get up then.' He'd found something to do and then we all got up and we all whipped ourselves with sticks and we all galloped through the town like Genghis Khan; like the great hordes from Tartar. And that was our game. The game slipped into this sense of winter. We galloped round the corner and down to the farm and then we galloped down to the pond, skimming across the ice and looking down at the bubbles of bullrushes and lilies waiting for summer to release them. I could never skate but all the idiots in the village seemed to be able to skate on one foot. They'd go sliding and gliding by and I'd always fall on my face and I thought, those drummondry louts, once you put them on ice they become Nureyev, they become star ballet dancers. Winter brought out that star quality.

But then in summer, summer was a time for playing the moon and the whole of the valley became our playground, and we'd run and run. We had a game called fox and hounds, and some of the lads would start off, we'd give them perhaps five or ten minutes and then we'd follow them. Starting in the village and running up through the valley galloping up through the woods. You were allowed to shout one thing: 'Whistle or holla or we shall not follow.' And they had to answer or we didn't know where they were. 'Whistle or holla or we shall not follow.' And then you'd hear, right up the valley, some little disguised call showing where they were and we'd go after them. Those sort of games and the moon, running with the mad hares on the top of the hill.

And I've tried to remember and have often remembered the quality of those moonlit nights, which had a quality of such unmoving and immortal stillness and excitement, with a full moon hanging above Swift's Hill. Rising tides in one's brain of Slad and summer, which linger there even now. That was summer. Chaps going up through the street, saying to the ladies, 'Hot enough for yer then?' To be answered with a worn-out shriek. Dogs lying under rain butts, to get out of the heat. And we boys lying in the grass, listening to the loops of cuckoos going across the valley and not knowing what to do, having nothing to do. No ideas in our heads. Nothing moving except summer. This radiant luxury of stillness. There was nothing to do but summer.

Well having laid down and done nothing because there was nothing to do, summer, someone would say, 'Well let's go down the pond then.' So we'd get up and go down the pond, and halfway down there was a little village shop on the corner by the old Elizabethan house, the big house, where we'd buy some sherbet dabs. That is what I remember as being an element of a summer's day, to buy sherbet dabs with a liquorish tube in it. If you sucked it was all right but if you blew, the bag exploded and you choked in a sort of paroxysm of sherbet and people coughing all over the road.

Coming out of school, haymaking. We'd rush off to the farms and say, 'Can we help?' Anything to get out into the fields after a long day of timetables, I mean tables. And then going off, helping the men forking sheaves onto the wagons and then getting waylaid. It wasn't as deliberate as all that. We didn't go over there to be seduced, we went over there to be a man and to help the men with the haymaking. But there was always, well not always, a Rosie type in the grass, waiting to waylay one of we sturdy lads. That was their job, temptresses. Temptresses of summer, and this one stopped me. I wasn't looking for trouble but I got it. She said:

> 'I got somat to show ye then.'
> I said, 'You ain't.'
> 'I have. Come here.'

So I stuck my fork into the ringing ground and followed her like doom and we went down onto a wagon festooned with grasses and she beckoned me under the wagon where there lay a large stone jar. 'It's cider, you ain't to drink it though, not much of it at any rate.' So we unstopped it and I held it to my mouth. Never to be forgotten, that first long drink of golden fire. Wine of wild orchards. And of that valley and of that time and of Rosie's burning cheeks. Never to be forgotten or ever tasted again.

That's what haymaking meant to me, and that's what cider meant to me. That's why it got me into trouble. But it wasn't haymaking. The step, the first half step, towards willing, half-willing seduction and it taught me a lesson, that women are stronger than men. The valley was education, the valley taught us everything, we didn't have to go anywhere.

Then when I was seventeen I left the valley. But leaving is a thing that is normal with the young. They leave the home as they grow. The cottage is like a nest. They grow and they fill it and there are too many of them and then they go off to see the world, make their fortune. They have to do that. I think it is an instinctual movement, to go out, leave home and see the world, and then possibly send money orders back to your mum. When you've made it.

And I went off one summer's morning and walked. I'd never seen the sea so I walked south to Southampton, then along the south coast and up into London and worked on a building site. I remember somebody saying, when anybody leaves home they always end up working on a building site, well I did. Then when that job was over I went to Spain for a year, with my violin. And that was one of the most carefree, happiest times of my life, discovering this almost medieval

Spain which in many ways reminded me of home. It was all horse traffic in Spain, horses and mules, and I was leaving a village which was all horses and mules and chaps sitting round and gossiping at night, and that sort of community which I'd left still existed. So it was a natural thing to do I think. I went to about forty countries while I was away: the Middle East, Africa and to Mexico. But I knew that I would have to come back here.

As a child I used to think that all the world was like this valley. This is the world. Born and the eyes open, you immediately register what you see, and I registered this uniquely beautiful valley and I thought this is life, everything's like this. And I didn't realize until I'd gone to all these other countries that nothing is like this. When I came back I thought, no I don't want to go again, I don't want to move again, I'm here, I'm rooted, I'm back.

The graveyard is opposite The Woolpack. I have been fortunate to survive this long and to survive very difficult crises abroad but I've got back and now it's all wrapped up. I drink in the pub and when I go, I will go across the road, or I'll be taken across the road in a box and put in the churchyard. And it's the comfort of peas in a pod again. I'm wrapped up in this little pod which is my home.

Down in the Valley

I've found a place halfway up the churchyard, which is near enough to the church to be aware of, in the spiritual sense, to be conscious of matins, Sunday morning, but also to be within reach of, in a temporal way, orgies on Saturday nights in The Woolpack. And alternating between the temporal and the spiritual is the way I wish to spend what eternity is left to me.

Afterword

This book has its origins in a series of conversations I recorded with Laurie Lee in and around Slad, his home village in the Cotswolds, in the spring and summer of 1994, Laurie's eightieth year. The recordings were the raw material for a television documentary film I was making, a film that various people, including Laurie himself, told me it would be impossible to achieve.

My initial request to Laurie, by letter, went to him via his agent in March 1994. About two weeks later, I came home from work and, as usual, played messages on the answerphone. The greeting on the machine had been recorded by my younger son in his high-pitched, unbroken ten-year-old voice: 'I'm sorry, but David, Joel and Louis can't take your call at the moment, but if you leave a message we'll get back to you as soon as possible.' Then, incredulously, I listened to the first message: 'That's a very nice answerphone message, if I may say so. Could you tell your daddy that Laurie Lee called him.'

Tentatively, I dialled the number he left. A voice answered in a soft, lilting Cotswold burr. It was Laurie Lee, talking to me! He said again how much he had liked the message on the answerphone, and asked me what I wanted of him. I told him pretty much what I had said to his agent. His tone was one of caution, but he suggested I drive out to meet him in his local pub, The Woolpack in Slad.

It was a bright, clear March day as I drove up the narrow lane from Stroud. It twisted and turned up the side of the valley and into the village. Laurie was sitting in his favourite spot in the bar of The Woolpack when I arrived, with half a pint of best and a whisky.

After we had talked for a while, I told him I wanted to make a half-hour film about him and the landscapes which had shaped his writing, such as the one I had just driven through: he was thoughtful, humorous and self-deprecating. In the end he said that he would help me as much as he could to make the film but that he did not want to be in it. Taken aback, I said that it would be impossible to make the film I had in mind if it did not include him, but he was adamant. By now we had finished our drinks.

'Do you have a car?' he asked. 'Then come with me.'

We got into the car and spent a glorious afternoon driving to some of the places that had a special meaning for him and which had shaped his writing. He took me to the village pond in Slad, to Miserden, Swift's Hill and Bulls Cross. In each place we got out of the car and he recounted a story associated with the place. I was mesmerized by his storytelling. I said that if I had had a camera I could have made the film there and then.

Towards the end of the afternoon Laurie repeated that he'd like to help me make the film but that he did not want to appear in it. How to solve the problem? I suggested a compromise. Suppose I came back to do pretty much what we had done that afternoon but this time with a sound recordist and a tape recorder. We would record our conversation, but only on sound; no pictures. He said that he would be happy with that arrangement. We parted having agreed a date, a Saturday in early April, when I would return. The day went extremely well. Laurie enjoyed himself and suggested I record him on film.

I filmed Laurie in eight different locations in the Slad Valley, the small area of the Cotswolds, north of Stroud, which shaped his early life and his later poetry and prose. We ranged over a host of themes. He talked about family, childhood, writing, music, politics, poetry, local characters and local history and, again and again, the landscape: its villages, steep valleys, fast-flowing streams. He came back continually to the ways in which the valley had shaped his writing.

The film we produced, 'Laurie Lee's Gloucestershire – A Writer's Landscape', was transmitted by HTV West on 21 August 1994, and subsequently by Channel 4 to commemorate Laurie's death in May 1997.

After transmission I filed the 'rushes', the tapes containing the recordings, and went on to other work. I always had it in mind to publish the recordings, but when I came to pay serious attention to the idea I couldn't find them. For a while I thought that I had inadvertently destroyed them. Then, in late 2017 I came across them in an incorrectly labelled archive box. This book is the result of that rediscovery.

The film I made with Laurie and the subsequent book would not have been possible without the help of Jeremy Payne, Bob Pitt, Peter Moseley, Chris Chapman, Anisa Farries, Joel Parker, Louis Parker, Melanie Nieuwenhuys and Claudio Ahlers, who assisted with recordings, and, subsequently, Colin Thomas, Jessy Lee, Norah Perkins, Thomas Penn, Richard Mason and, for his careful reading of the text and many helpful suggestions, John Richmond.

David Parker
Bristol, June 2019